FIELD NOTEBOOKS

HOW SCIENTISTS RECORD AND WRITE ABOUT OBSERVATIONS

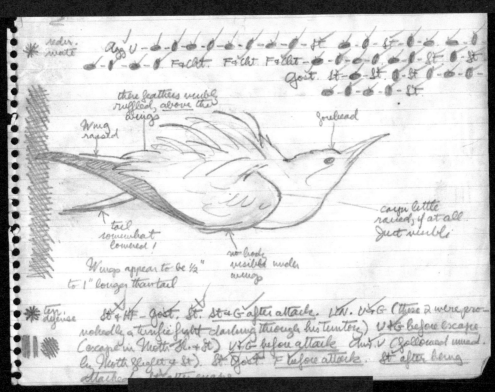

DARCY PATTISON

WHAT ARE FIELD NOTEBOOKS?

RECORDING OBSERVATIONS

Field notebooks are places where scientists record observations when they are out in the field. That means they are not sitting in an office or a laboratory. Instead, they are in a field, a meadow, a cave, or wherever they need to be to make their observations in nature.

WHAT DO THEY WRITE?

Some field notebooks read like a diary, with the scientist recording the day's events and what they thought about them.

Others simply record lists of specimens collected and information about them.

To share the information, scientists publish it in many ways.

TEXT, IMAGES, OR BOTH?

Until recently, there were just two ways to record observations: text and images.

TEXT

A field notebook's text, or the words, can be informational, a narrative, or a description. The text can be brief, such as a simple list. Or it can be many pages of description of a journey. Or, it can include measurements.

NAME	NO.	DATE
Gull, Laughing (*Larus Atricilla*)	58	June 22, 1936
Tern, Gull Billed (*Gelochelidon Nilotica*)	63	June 26, 1936
Tern, Common (*Sterna Hirundo*)	70	June 26, 1936
Skimmer, Black (*Rynchops Nigra*)	80	June 24, 1936

Joshua F. B. Camblos wrote a list of birds and the dates he saw them.

IMAGES

Images were traditionally drawn into notebooks, but as technology improved, some scientists added photographs. Sometimes, the images stand alone. More often, they are labeled with measurements, date, time, or other information. Captions may be used to explain something, or sometimes you need to read the text to understand the image. Color can be included in images to add information.

IN CANE-GRASS. FEB 7.

TEXT AND IMAGES

Abel Chapman added a caption to this elephant drawing made during a trip to Sudan in 1913:

"IN CANE-GRASS. FEB 7."

ALEXANDER WETMORE

1886–1978
Ornithologist (bird scientist)
Born in North Freedom, Wisconsin

FEBRUARY, 1904 – BIRD LIST.

- Bluejay
- Hairy Woodpecker
- English Sparrow
- White-breasted Nuthatch
- Chicadee
- Downy Woodpecker
- Crow
- Great Horned Owl
- Junco
- Tree Sparrow
- Ruffed Grouse
- Barred Owl
- Screech Owl
- Bobwhite
- American Goldfinch
- Pine Grosbeak
- Prairie Horned Lark
- Brown Creeper
- Redpoll
- Evening Grosbeak
- American Goshawk
- Acadian Owl
- Bohemian Waxwing
- American Crossbill

24

WRITING LISTS

Wetmore had a simple idea for his journals. He just made lists of birds he saw in a single month. Other scientists list ideas, equipment, observations, what they saw, or what they heard.

BIRD LOVER

Alexander Wetmore started writing in his journals when he was 8-years-old. His family went on vacation to Florida, where he saw a pelican and wrote about it. By age 14, he was writing monthly lists of birds that he saw.

Wetmore's first job was for the US Bureau of Biological Survey. He studied birds in Latin America and Puerto Rico. For two years, he traveled in South America. He studied bird migration from North America to South America. Later, he studied the food habits of North American birds.

Wetmore worked for the Smithsonian Institution from 1924 to 1952. He led the Smithsonian as its sixth Secretary from 1945 to 1952. During the Great

Depression of the 1930s, he struggled to keep as many people working as possible. World War II (1939-1945) made it hard to travel to study birds. Instead, Wetmore studied the birds of the Shenandoah National Park in Virginia.

After World War II ended, Wetmore could travel more to study birds. For 20 years, from 1946 to 1966, he made yearly trips to Panama. In 1965, Wetmore published *The Birds of the Republic of Panama*. He wrote about 189 species and sub-species of birds that were new to science.

Wetmore also studied and wrote over 150 scientific papers about bird fossils.

Fifty-six new genera, species, and subspecies of birds (both recent and fossil) were named in his honor. Other animals named for him included mammals, amphibians, insects, and mollusks. Wetmore jokingly called these his "private zoo."

All his life, Wetmore wrote in his notebooks. He listed birds and other animals he saw in his travels. He also used photography and left several photo albums of his work.

A YOUNG AUTHOR

In this October 1901 photograph, Wetmore holds a copy of his first published article, "My Experience with a Red-headed Woodpecker," which appeared in the October 1900 *Bird-Lore* magazine. It describes watching a woodpecker store acorns for winter.

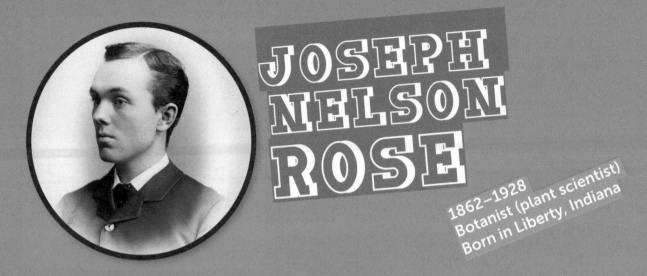

JOSEPH NELSON ROSE

1862–1928
Botanist (plant scientist)
Born in Liberty, Indiana

CACTUS LOVER

Joseph Rose spent a lifetime describing plants. While at Wabash College in Indiana, Rose learned to classify plants. He helped classify herbs such as dill, caraway, fennel, and coriander.

In 1883, he moved his wife and six children to Washington, D.C. There, he worked as an assistant botanist at the US Department of Agriculture. He began studying plants of Mexico and Central America, specializing in cacti. He visited Mexico nine times on collection trips and sent back many live specimens, which were grown in greenhouses. Some of the cacti he collected are still alive.

Rose co-authored a four-volume book, *The Cactaceae*, with Nathaniel Lord Britton. To write the book, Rose and Britton traveled across Europe to visit herbariums. An herbarium is any collection of dried plants that are arranged in some order. They also traveled to Argentina, Bolivia, Brazil, Chile, Ecuador, Peru, Venezula, and the West Indies.

Rose helped name and describe 972 species of cactus. To do this, he looked at all the similar species. Next, he described the new species carefully. He made sure the description was different from other similar cacti. In Rose's lifetime, he published over 200 scientific articles. He co-wrote with at least 12 other botanists on various projects.

DESCRIPTIVE WRITING

Not all observations are done in the wild. The notes above are a careful observation of a blooming cactus in a greenhouse. Many of the words, or vocabulary, used are scientific ways of describing a plant. For example, a *bract* is a leaf that has a special purpose. Rose used descriptive writing to talk about the flower.

Size: "flower 3.5 cm long, about 1.5 cm in diameter"

Shape: "petals numerous, oblong elliptical, jagged"

Color: "glistening creamy white on inside, same on outside save for narrow purple stripe at center"

Number: "separated into 7 green stigma lobes"

Place collected: "Northern Mexico by C.A. Purpus in 1905."

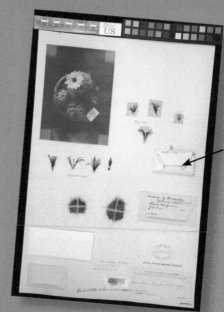

Envelope for seeds.

DRYING PLANTS

Most plant specimens are preserved by drying, so they don't rot as easily. Plant presses are built to squeeze a plant until the water is taken out. Plants are placed between absorbent papers. Usually, a press has screws to squeeze the plant tighter and tighter. Scientists might dry the whole plant, or they might dry a plant part, like a flower. As the specimen dries, the papers are changed often.

After a plant is dried, it's mounted on heavy paper. The goal is to show as much of the plant as possible for future studies. Notice that the photo shows envelopes holding seeds.

WILLIAM & LUCILE MANN

LUCILE: 1897–1986
Writer and editor
Born in Ann Arbor, Michigan

WILLIAM: 1886–1960
Entomologist (insect scientist)
zoologist, and zookeeper
Born in Helena, Montana

ANIMAL LOVERS

As a child, William Mann loved animals. Once, he tried to run away and join a circus. At 17 years old, he worked briefly at the National Zoological Park in Washington, D.C. He cleaned animal cages. Many years later, in 1925, he became the Superintendent of the National Zoological Park. He led many expeditions to collect live animals for the zoo.

During World War I, Lucile Quarry worked in military intelligence in Washington, D.C. By 1922, she was an editor for *The Woman's Home Companion* magazine.

Lucile and William married in 1926. Lucile often traveled with William on expeditions to collect live animals. Once, she had to hide a bag of live snakes under her skirts while on a train trip. She was a member of the Society of Woman Geographers.

One big trip to collect animals was the 1937 National Geographic Society-Smithsonian Institution Expedition to visit what are now India, Malaysia, Singapore, Sumatra and Thailand.

DIARY OR NARRATIVE WRITING

Lucile Mann kept a typed diary, or a narrative, of their 1937 collection trip. In Singapore, Lucile wrote about the city. A syce is a stable attendant. A sampan is a kind of boat. Sikhs are people from a religious group of India. Tamils are a people group from Sri Lanka, then part or India. A zebu is a hump-backed cow used to pull carts.

As we drove back to the hotel, I tried to count the smells of Singapore: Incense, fried fish, wood smoke, the oil on the syce's hair, roasting peanuts, the scent of flowers, the smoke of firecrackers which the Chinese are always putting off, and occasional unsanitary whiffs better not analysed.

We were sorry to leave this fascinating city, with its mixture of races, its crowded harbor, and the waterways where so many people live their lives in sampans; traffic policemen with rattan boards on their back for stop and go signs; sikhs and tamils from India directing the traffic of every imaginable Asiatic people; zebu carts rubbing axles with the latest make of motor car; orchids a customary decoration on the table.

When scientists make observations, they often pay attention to their senses. They write about what they see, hear, smell, taste, and touch (temperature and texture, not feelings).

For example, Lucile listed eight things she smelled in Singapore.

LIFE AT THE ZOO

As the wife of a zookeeper, Lucile became familiar with orphaned or sickly animal babies. When needed, the Manns brought home baby animals to feed them and take care of them. This tiger cub was named Babette.

FRED LOWE SOPER

1893–1977
Epidemiologist (scientist who studies the source and cause of infectious diseases)
Born in Hutchinson, Kansas

PREVENTATIVE MEDICINE

Fred Soper was a public health doctor. In January 1920, after his medical training, Soper started work at the Rockefeller Foundation. He started his career in public health at a time when people across the globe were affected by major diseases such as hookworm infection, tuberculosis, malaria, influenza, typhus fever, and yellow fever.

Among the Rockefeller projects was the International Health Division (IHD). The IHD had worked to eradicate, or completely destroy, hookworms in the American South from 1909 to 1914. In 1910, over 40% of people had hookworms, a worm that can live and grow in human intestines. When the IHD hookworm eradication program was successful, the IHD decided to repeat the program in other countries.

Soper worked in Brazil from 1920-1927 to control hookworm infections. Starting in 1927, he worked to stop malaria and yellow fever by killing the mosquitoes that carried these diseases. Some people called Soper the "Mosquito Killer." One tool to kill mosquitoes was a new man-made chemical called DDT. Many called DDT a lifesaver because it killed so many mosquitoes. However, DDT had unexpected environmental effects and was banned in 1972. Today, we still have many diseases carried by mosquitoes, such as the Zika virus. The public fight for healthy living conditions continues.

WRITING WITH HUMOR

In 1922, Soper visited the city of Sertão, Brazil. There, he learned a startling thing. Recently, the city had had a big party to celebrate its first public latrine. A latrine is a community bathroom. Usually, it was made by digging a hole in the ground.

Latrines were an important part of fighting hookworms. Hookworms live and grow in the intestines of people. When an infected person goes to the bathroom, the hookworm's eggs come out, too. The eggs hatch and become larvae. The larvae can enter people through the bottoms of their feet. People walking barefoot in unclean areas can easily be infected with hookworms. Latrines meant the hookworm eggs weren't spread in the soil.

In his diary, Soper joked that a celebration party was a "new idea." He made a promise: if the region opened at least 10 new latrines, Soper would make the four-day journey to join the next party. Sometimes scientists write funny things in their notebooks!

HOOKWORMS AND TAPEWORMS
This 9-year-old Brazilian boy is holding a board with the hookworms and tapeworms that he expelled.

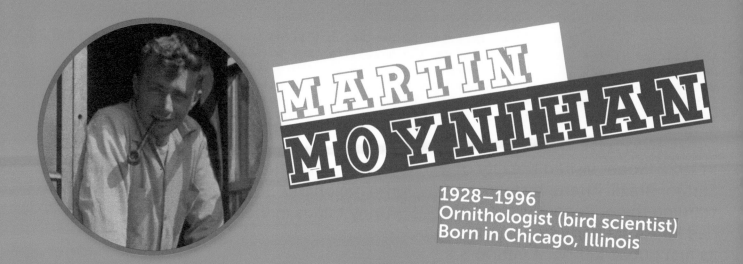

MARTIN MOYNIHAN

1928–1996
Ornithologist (bird scientist)
Born in Chicago, Illinois

BLACK AND WHITE DRAWINGS

As a child, Martin Moynihan traveled in Europe. He learned to speak French, German, and Spanish. Moynihan became interested in birds at age 15. He published his first scientific paper by age 18.

Moynihan worked in Panama from 1957 to 1974. He helped build the Smithsonian Tropical Research Institute on Barro Colorado Island. To build the Panama Canal, some rivers were dammed to make Gatun Lake. That meant the existing tropical forest was covered with water. Only the tallest hills remained above water as islands. Barro Colorado Island is one of those islands. It's become one of the most studied tropical forests in the world.

The institute studied biological diversity and tropical ecology. Biological diversity is the study of how many and what kinds of plants or animals are found in a certain area. An area with lots of different kinds of plants or animals has a high biological diversity. Tropical ecology is the relationship between living things and the environment in the tropic zones.

Moynihan's notebooks were always with him. He was known for black-and-white ink drawings of his subjects. Sometimes they were published as part of his scientific papers. Underwater, he carried a waterproof notebook to take notes about squids.

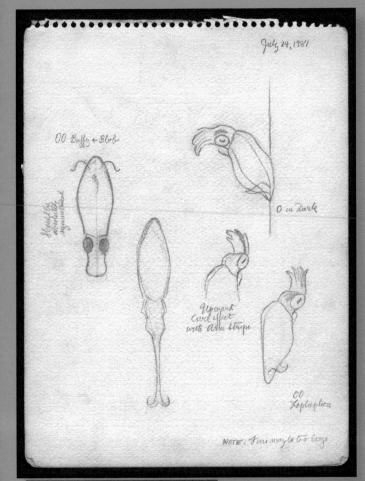

ORGANIZING FIELD NOTES

Moynihan carefully dated each entry in his field notes. The dates created a strong chronological order. The newest entries were added to the back of each notebook. However, every couple of years, he reorganized his notebooks. He put information about a single species into a folder. Then he renumbered the pages. This reorganization was topical. A topical order means the notes were organized by information about a topic, usually a certain animal.

Moynihan often drew in his notebooks. On November 13, 1955, he labeled parts of a South American gull. The note on the bottom left says, "*Wings appear to be ½" to 1" longer than tail.*"

Moynihan liked to use question marks and exclamation points!

DRAWING SPECIMENS

Sometimes, Moynihan wrote notes around his drawings.

The first one above says, "Should be absolutely symmetrical." *Symmetrical* means that if you fold the squid in half, both sides should look the same. It's hard to draw exactly symmetrical, so his note would remind him of his observation.

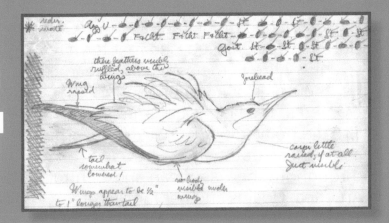

MARGARET S. COLLINS

1922–1996
Entomologist (insect scientist)
Born in Institute, West Virginia

SCIENCE AND CIVIL RIGHTS

Margaret S. Collins was the first African American woman to earn a Ph.D. in entomology, or the study of insects. She became known as the Termite Lady.

Collins was considered a child prodigy, and at age 6, she was allowed to check out books from the West Virginia State College Library. She skipped two grades and graduated from high school at age 14.

While working on her Ph.D. at the University of Chicago, she met termite scientist Alfred Emerson, who became her mentor. However, he thought that women in the field were "annoying." She did no field work until she became a professor, but then she traveled throughout the Caribbean and Central America. Collins and her family often visited the Everglades, where she collected specimens. Together with David Nickle, she identified a new species of termite called *Neotermes luykxi.*

In addition to her scientific work, Collins was also a civil rights activist, participating in the Tallahassee bus boycott in 1956.

After a career of teaching, Collins worked at the Smithsonian Institution, organizing its termite collection. She died on a 1996 collection trip to the Cayman Islands.

RECORDING STATISTICS

Recording numbers for observations is important. Collins counted termites, recorded dates and times, and noted how those numbers changed over time.

REPEATED OBSERVATIONS

Collins studied how termites fight. In 1982, she visited Suriname, a small South American country. She often made observations over time to understand behavior.

On August 28, 1982, Collins watched a territorial battle between different kinds of termites. She wrote the following notes:

Brown Heads vs. Constrictotermes

5 soldiers + 5 workers of each

After 15 minutes:

Brown heads: 4 injured workers, 3 on back. 2 injured soldiers.

Constricto: 1 injured worker, 0 injured soldiers.

DRAWING COLONY MAPS

Collins often added drawings to her notes about termite battles. First, she drew large circles to show the two termite colonies, along with a key to explain her smaller symbols. Here, the small inked circles are brown head soldiers (circle with line) and workers (circle). The yellow head soldiers and workers are shown in lighter-colored pencil.

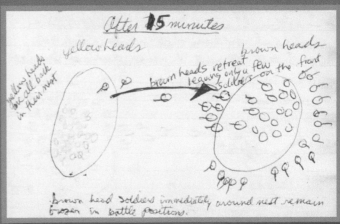

Notice that this drawing is after 15 minutes of battle. After 25 minutes, Collins wrote: "Brown heads are again on yellow head nest. Basically everything is a standoff. Both species still have *complete* control of their nest it's just that the brown heads seem to be a little more full of adventure, spying or the surveying the situation because they are always scuttling back and forth between nests but yet never going for enough to engage in anything greater than rare squirting exchange." (NOTE: In fights, temites often squirt acid from their foreheads.)

Collins used text and art to explain her observations. She drew a map showing the opening positions, and then new maps as the battle continued. The last map is at 40 minutes. Recording information over time allowed her to follow the battle's progress .

WILLIAM DALL

1845 - 1927
Malacologist (mollusk scientist) and naturalist
Born in Boston, Massachusetts

EXPLORING ALASKA

In 1865, Alaska was owned by Russia. It was called Russian America. Not much was known about these frozen lands. But technology changed all that. In 1858, the Western Union Telegraph Company placed the first undersea cable across the Atlantic Ocean. By 1861, the eastern United States was linked to the West Coast by telegraph. After that success, Western Union decided to start a new project. They wanted to lay telegraph cable from San Francisco, California, to Moscow, Russia. They planned to go through Alaska.

As part of the Western Union Telegraph Expedition, 20-year-old William Dall traveled north. His scientific interests were mainly in malacology, or the study of mollusks. The mollusk family includes snails, slugs, clams, octopuses, and squids. Dall kept a diary of his travels through Alaska and across the Bering Sea to Russia. While the expedition was in Alaska, they received exciting news. On March 30, 1867, the United States had bought Alaska from Russia. They paid $7.2 million. In 1959, Alaska became the 49th state of the United States.

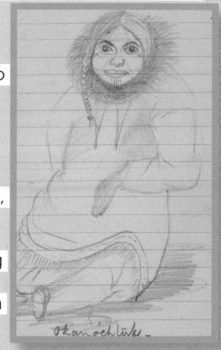

okan'óchluks

LOCAL POTTERY AT ANVIK

In this drawing, can you guess how much liquid each pot holds? This is an example of when text and images are both needed to understand information

From Dall's diary entry for Thursday, July 18, 1867. "See for the first time pottery made by Indians and the only pottery made in the country. Very large pots of canteen holding from five gallons to half a gallon and a rude cup with two lumps of clay as handles...".

The large pot held five gallons, the medium pot held about half a gallon, and smallest pot held about one cup.

DRAWING PEOPLE (left)

This is a sketch of an Alaskan native woman whom Dall met in Ulukuk. It shows the warm clothing needed in Alaska.

DRAWING MAPS

Dall drew this map of the Alaskan region where they were traveling. It shows rivers and place names written in the local language. He included special marks to help him remember how to say the words correctly.

DONALD S. ERDMAN

1919 - 2002
Ichthyologist (fish scientist)
Born in New York, New York

QUAKER

Little is known about Donald Erdman's personal life. He was a conscientious objector during World War II. As a Quaker, he believed in peace and not fighting. He would not become a soldier. Instead, the government let such men work in the Civilian Public Service program. He worked in Massachusetts, New York, New Hampshire, and finally, Puerto Rico, where he did public health work. This was likely Erdman's first time in Puerto Rico. He later returned to live and work there.

FISH IN THE PERSIAN GULF

After World War II, Erdman served as a scientific aide in the Division of Fishes, United States National Museum (USNM). In 1948, he joined a fisheries survey of the Persian Gulf and Red Sea. The Arabian American Oil Company (ARAMCO) wanted to know more about local fish. Perhaps, they could buy local fish to feed their employees. Erdman collected nearly 5,000 fish specimens for the USNM. For most, he wrote down the English name and the Arabic name. After the survey, ARAMCO decided to buy more fish from local Arab fishermen.

During his trip to the Persian Gulf for ARAMCO, Erdman kept a journal. He wrote, "The Persian Gulf and Red Sea can in summer be the hottest seas in the world."

Vast sun-baked deserts surrounded the area. The deserts helped heat up the water. In August 1948, Erdman recorded an open water temperature of 104°F (40°C).

COLOR ADDS INFOMRATION

LEFT: Erdman drew a spangled emperor fish (*Lethrinus nebulosus*), and used color to help describe the fish. When the fish were preserved, they turned dark brown or black. Erdman explained that the colors were spread out except the purple-blue spots on the head. The top was light steel-blue color, mixed in with yellow. Faint black bands seemed to be at random.

DRAW, THEN WRITE

Erdman often drew a fish on his page and then wrote around the drawing. By putting his drawing in the middle of a page, he could explain the drawing so the text and drawing worked together. He added color to help identify the fish.

MARY AGNES CHASE

1869-1963
Botanist (plant scientist),
suffragist working for women's rights, and author
Born in Wady Petra, Illinois

GRASSES

In 1893, Mary Agnes Chase visited the World's Columbian Exposition in Chicago, Illinois. It inspired her to study plants and grasses. She became a botanical illustrator, drawing plants.

Chase studied grasses in the United States, Europe, Central America, and South America.

IMAGE: Mary Agnes Chase and Brazilian botanist Maria do Carmo Bandeira on a mountain top. Chase set records for a woman climbing the highest mountains in Brazil.

FIG. 1. Vegetative part of a grass plant; part of leaf opened out.

DRAWING SPECIMEN - CLOSE UPS

Chase began her career as a botanical illustrator in Chicago. When she moved to Washington, DC, in 1903, her job was drawing more plants. The careful study needed to draw plants, though, meant she learned a lot about them. Even more study meant she became an expert on grasses.

Chase drew many of the specimens that she collected. Often, she used a microscope to see the tiny structures.

By drawing, instead of photographing, Chase could include both the roots and the plant. Notice that she also included a close-up of the grass joints. Labels add even more information. For her book, *First Book of Grasses,* she included many illustrations like this.

SNAKE!
In a 1929 journal, Chase wrote about her travel to climb the western side of the Caparaó Mountain range in Brazil. She hoped to find new grasses. She joked, "One who has been to Brazil is expected to tell about snakes, so I am glad to have at least this big one." About eight feet away, she saw a 15-foot snake. Its head was raised two feet off the ground. She wrote, "I backed off respectfully."

WILLIAM HENRY HOLMES

1846-1933
Anthropologist, archaeologist, artist, and explorer
Born in Cadiz, Ohio

EXPLORER, GEOLOGIST, ARCHAEOLOGIST, AND ARTIST

William Henry Holmes is always described as an explorer. He worked in geology and archaeology, but his career began at the Smithsonian Institution, where he drew fossils and shells of live mollusks. A trip to Yellowstone National Park in 1872 established him as a scientific illustrator, cartographer (mapmaker), geologist (rock scientist) and archaeologist (scientist who studies early human history).

He became known for his paintings of Yellowstone, the Grand Canyon, Mesa Verde, and Mayan ruins in Mexico. Holmes also focused on Native American pottery and textiles.

Holmes was skilled as a mountain climber, and two mountains were named after him: Mount Holmes, in Yellowstone National Park, and Mount Holmes, in the Henry Mountains of Utah.

Holmes worked at the Field Museum of Natural History in Chicago for a time and taught anthorpology at the University of Chicago. Later, he worked for the United States National Musuem at the Smithsonian Institution. In 1920, he became director of the National Gallery of Art, now the Smithsonian American Art Museum. One of his special projects was to assemble exhibits of Native American arts and objects.

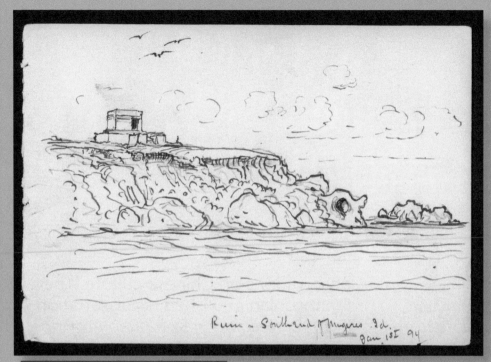

CAPTION: Ruin - South end of Mujeres Id. Jan 1st 94

DRAWING LANDSCAPES
CAPTION: Ruin - South end of Mujeres Island, January 1, 1894.

Shown in the drawing is Isla Mujeres, or the Island of Women, an island off the Yucatan Peninsula in Mexico. The Mayan people traditionally considered it a sacred island dedicated to Ixchel, the goddess of childbirth and medicine. This drawing shows how the ruins of her temple looked over 100 years ago.

In 1988, Hurricane Gilbert destroyed most of the temple leaving only the foundations. That makes this an important historical drawing.

DRAWING PEOPLE
This is a drawing of some women Holmes saw on Isla Mujeres.

LANDSCAPE OF BIRDS
Near the Maya ruins, Holmes drew this landscape, which shows cranes, plovers, kingfishers, flamingoes, vultures, hawks, and other birds.

DAVID CROCKETT GRAHAM

1884-1961
Missionary and naturalist
Born in Green Forest, Arkansas

GLOBAL DIVERSITY

David Graham served as a Christian missionary in China for 37 years from 1911 to 1948. During his travels in the country, he collected and shipped to the Smithsonian Institution over 400,000 specimens of mammals, birds, insects, and snakes, including 230 new species. Over 29 species were named after him. In 1929, Graham was made a Fellow of the Royal Geographical Society. In 1931, the Smithsonian named him a "Collaborator in Biology."

Graham's field notebooks follow his 14 journeys collecting specimens in Szechuan Province. During Graham's time in China, the country was in political turmoil. He often hired armed guards for his travels. Besides collecting specimens, Graham also recorded his observations on Chinese culture. The Smithsonian published his dissertation in 1928, *Religion in Szechuan Province, China.* He also sent back costumes and handicrafts from local ethnic minority groups.

From 1932 to 1948, Graham lived in Chengdu, China, and taught archaeology and anthropology at the West China Union University. After his retirement, Graham wrote three books about ethnic minority groups and their songs, culture, and religion, all published by the Smithsonian.

PANDAS FOR THE BRONX ZOO

In 1941, Madame Chiang Kai-shek, the wife of the Chinese leader, wanted to send a thank-you gift for America's support during the war with Japan.

MAP OF THE
NINGYUENFU TRIP
1928
D.C. GRAHAM

Part of Diary #4

1928 COLLECTING TRIP

In 1928, Graham visited the area north of Suifu (now called Yibin), where he lived. The map is difficult to understand today because the names of cities and locations have changed. However, on his handdrawn maps, Graham included approximate longitude and latitude lines which helps place the map in context.

Graham's curiosity drove him to look carefully at the people and the land, while also concentrating on collecting specimens. For example, on July 7, 1928, he visited a Han dynasty burial cave, stopped at a coal mine to study how they removed water from the mine, and crossed four rivers. The next day, he spoke at three local churches. On July 9, it stormed, and the muddy roads delayed Graham's travel.

He wrote:
"On account of rain and wind the catch of insects is small. Secured one bird. It seems to me that my richest catch in specimens during the past few months has been in bees, wasps, etc."

At her request, Graham hired 70 hunters with 40 dogs to search for pandas. He wrote that it was "probably the biggest panda hunt ever organized at one time."

They eventually caught two female pandas. Graham wrote, "Missionaries sometimes have to tackle strange and unusual jobs." The pandas arrived safely at the Bronx Zoo in New York City on December 30, 1941.

WATSON M. PERRYGO

1906-1984
Taxidermist, field collector, and exhibits specialist
Born in Washington, D.C.

TAXIDERMIST

Watson Perrygo became interested in natural history as a teenager when he started visiting the Smithsoian Institution's United States National Musuem (USNM). At the time, Alexander Wetmore was the director of the Smithsonian, and he took Perrrygo on birding trips with him.

As a teenager, Perrygo saw an advertisement on a matchbox for a special class. It was for a correspondence course to learn taxidermy. Taxidermy is the art of preserving and mounting animal skins to make them look lifelike. Taxidermy was an important part of collecting specimens. Plants and animals will rot unless preserved. Today, preserved specimens are the only way to study some extinct species.

Perrygo started working at the Smithsonian in 1927 as a scientific aide. Later, he worked as a taxidermist. He never worked anywhere else.

Perrygo went on many collection trips across the United States, Haiti, and Panama. He also updated many musuem exhibits

To share information from field work, Perrygo and others at the Smithsonian wrote information labels about each exhibit. Sometimes they read scientists' notebooks or talked to the scientists about the specimen. They needed to know about the species, where it was collected, and any observations the scientists had made. Then, they used informative writing to explain exhibits.

SHARING INFORMATION—INFORMATIVE WRITING

This photo shows taxidermists mounting a hippopotamus for exhibition at the USNM in the 1930s. Perrygo is third from the left. Because the hippopotamus is a water animal, it was especially hard to prepare the skin.

Here's the informational text that accompanied the hippopotamus exhibit:

The "hippo" or "river horse" formerly occurred in all prominent rivers, streams, pools, and lakes, throughout Africa south of the Sahara. Today this animal is found only in larger bodies of water. Living in herds of from a few to many individuals, hippos spend their days lying partly or wholly submerged in water while at night they go on land along well-established pathways to graze. Although the hippo looks harmless, old males may be vicious. They have been known to attack canoes and small boats and smash them with their enormous jaws.

GEORGE WASHINGTON CARVER

1864-1943
Chemist, agriculture professor, and inventor
Born in Diamond Grove, Missouri

SCIENTIST AND WRITER

George Washington Carver was born as an enslaved person near the end of the Civil War. He later attended Iowa State Agricultural College and became its first African American graduate with both a bachelor's degree and a master's degree.

In 1896, the Tuskegee Institute president Booker T. Washington recruited Carver to become the head of the institute's Agriculture Department. Carver taught there for 47 years. He was the most famous African American scientist of the early 20th century.

In 1897, Alabama passed a law to create "...two Branch Agricultural Experiment Stations for the Colored Race..." One station would be in Tuskegee, Alabama.

As part of the Tuskegee Agricultural Experiment Station, Carver wrote 44 bulletins that reported the experiments and field work of the station. Each bulletin had practical farming advice. The first one discussed how acorns fatten up wild hogs. Five bulletins talked about growing cotton, the cash crop of the South. Others included recipes.

In 1906, Carver designed a Jessup wagon, a laboratory on wheels. It traveled around Alabama to help educate farmers about growing crops.

Carver was a Christian who easily combined faith and science in his life and often led Bible studies with students. In his speaking, he worked for racial harmony and met with three U.S. presidents: Theodore Roosevelt, Calvin Coolidge, and Franklin Roosevelt.

PUBLICATION–SHARING INFORMATION

Carver supervised the experimental farms and oversaw the planting, harvesting, and analysis of crops grown under different experimental conditions. To share the information, he wrote a series of bulletins. Often he included tables comparing different experimental conditions. Sometimes, he drew diagrams.

In the 1916 *Bulletin 31: How to Grow the Peanut & 105 Ways of Preparing It for Human Consumption*. Carver gives 105 recipes for using peanuts. Unless people had good recipes for peanuts, they wouldn't buy them. The recipes made it easier for people to understand this food and figure out how to use it.

Carver also published recipes for cow peas, sweet potatoes, tomatoes, and wild plums.

DRAW, THEN ADD CAPTIONS

In his writing, Carver sometimes added a black-and-white drawing. This drawing explains to farmers how to help pollinate, a process that allows plants to grow seeds. Notice that he signed his drawing!

To identify parts of the plant, Carver wrote a letter of the alphabet and drew a line from the letter to part of the plant. Then, he created a key. A drawing or map key is a way to help people understand the drawing by explaining what each label means. Here, letter "a" means that the plant part is a flower. It may be a flower bud, or a flower bloom.

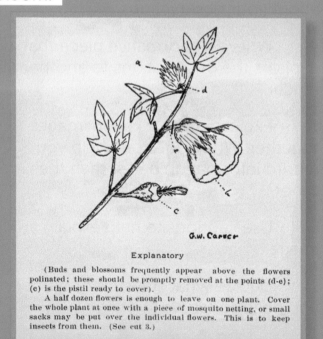

G.W. Carver

Explanatory

(Buds and blossoms frequently appear above the flowers polinated; these should be promptly removed at the points (d-e); (c) is the pistil ready to cover).

A half dozen flowers is enough to leave on one plant. Cover the whole plant at once with a piece of mosquito netting, or small sacks may be put over the individual flowers. This is to keep insects from them. (See cut 3.)

START YOUR OWN FIELD BOOK

1) Start with a simple list.

2) Describe what you observe. Use words that talk about what you see, hear, taste, smell, or feel (temperature and texture, not emotions). Learn scientific words to use.

3) Write a narrative or tell a true story about your observations.

4) Write an informative piece that explains the observations to another reader.

5) Explore using text and images together. When does one help you record information better than the other?

6) Use captions to help explain an image.

7) Decide what statistics or numbers you need to record.

8) Decide if you need to make observations over time.

9) Decide how you will organize your information. You might choose chronological or topical orders.

10) Use color to add information to an image.

11) Draw or photograph specimens.

12) Draw or photograph landscapes and people.

13) Draw a map. Could you give the same information with a photograph?

14) What current technology would help you record observations? Think about audio, text, or images.

15) How will you share or publish your observations? You could create an exhibit of specimens and label them. Or perhaps you want to write an article, print it, and give it to people.

FIELD NOTEBOOKS: How Scientists Record and Write About Observations
by Darcy Pattison

Text © 2021 Darcy Pattison
Selected sections were previously published as *My Steam Notebook*, Mims House, © 2016. Used by permission.

Mims House
1309 Broadway
Little Rock, AR 72202, USA
MimsHouseBooks.com

Publisher's Cataloging-in-Publication data

Names: Pattison, Darcy, author.
Title: Field notebooks : how scientists record and write about observations / by Darcy Pattison.
Description: Little Rock, AR: Mims House, 2021.
Identifiers: ISBN: 978-1-62944-191-7 (hardcover) | 978-1-62944-192-4 (paperback) | 978-1-62944-193-1 (ebook) | LCCN 2021907420
Subjects: LCSH Science--Methodology--Juvenile literature. | Scientists--Juvenile literature. | Science--Observations--Juvenile literature. | CYAC Science--Methodology. | Scientists. | BISAC JUVENILE NONFICTION / Science & Nature / General
Classification: LCC Q175.2 .P38 2021 | DDC 507.2--dc23

PHOTO PERMISSIONS

Random Records of a Lifetime Devoted to Science and Art, 1846-1931 (Freer Gallery, 1932); top right, top far right, and bottom right: Cozumel, Mexico, 1895. Courtesy of Smithsonian Institution Archives. Image # Holmes-Cozumel-SIA-SIA_007084_B03_F06-2, Holmes-Cozumel-SIA-SIA_007084_B03_F06, and Holmes-Birds-SIA-SIA_007084_B03_F06-3.

David Crockett Graham. Portrait: Courtesy of Chris Hoogendyk; right: Map of the Ninguenfu Trip, 1928. Courtesy of Smithsonian Institution Archives. Image # SIA2012-9992.

Watson M. Perrygo. Portrait: Watson M. Perrygo with Snake Specimen, 1929. Courtesy of Smithsonian Institution Archives. Image # 84-8050; right: Taxidermists Adjusting Hippopotamus Skin on Model Preparatory to Making Clay Model, 1927. Courtesy of Smithsonian Institution Archives. Image # SIA2012-6469.

George Washington Carver. Portrait: George Washington Carver Graduation Photo, 1893. Iowa State University Special Collections and University Archives. Call number: RS 21/7/A. Carver.V-01-01; top right: How to Grow the Peanut and 105 Ways of Preparing it for Human Consumption (Tuskegee Normal and Industrial Institute, May 1917), Bulletin No. 32, p. 10; bottom right: Cotton Growing for Rural Schools, (Tuskegee Normal and Industrial Institute, 1911), Bulletin No. 20, p. 26.

Dedication page. Abel Chapman, Sudan ii, 1912–1913. Courtesy of Smithsonian Institution Archives. Image #11913-Chap.

NOTES

Margaret Collins. Margaret Collins, Combat Data, Suriname, Notes, 1982, Smithsonian Institution Archives, SIA2017-037169 and SIA2017-037176, http://siarchives.si.edu/collections/fbr_item_modsi6567

William Dall. William Healey Dall, Diary July 14–November 30, 1867, Biodiversity Heritage Library, SIA RU007073, https://www.biodiversitylibrary.org/item/189992, p. 17.

Mary Agnes Chase. Mary Agnes Chase Trips to Brazil, 1925-1930, Smithsonian Institution Archives, SIA RU000229, https://ia800301.us.archive.org/29/items/MaryAgnesChaset00Chas/MaryAgnesChaset00Chas.pdf, p. 21-22

David Graham. David Graham in "How an American Missionary Helped Capture the First Panda Given to the U.S." by Colin Schulz, SmithsonianMag.com, August 18, 2014, https://www.smithsonianmag.com/smart-news/how-american-missionary-helped-captured-first-panda-given-us-180952369/. David Crockett Graham, Diary no. IV [4], July, 1928–August, 1928: Summer Expedition to Ningyuenfu via Yachow, Smithsonian Institution Archives, Image # SIA2012-8840, http://siarchives.si.edu/collections/fbr_item_modsi2133 .

Watson Perrygo. Hippopotamus, Hall of Mammals, National Museum of Natural History, Smithsonian Libraries and Archives, SIA#hippo-mnh217, https://www.si.edu/object/siris_sic_9902.

For Haileigh, Bruce, Zeke, Gabe, Ash, and Neona:

Always observe the good things in life.

Don't sleep through them!

Abel Chapman drew this sleeping hippopotamus in the Sudan on February 16, 1913.